YOU CAN I
70⁺ Truths about the Gift of Prophecy

- 30⁺ Reasons to Prophesy

- 10⁺ Ways to Prepare for Prophetic Words and Encounters

- 10⁺ Ways to Activate Prophetic Grace

- 10⁺ Ways to Obtain a Prophecy

- 10⁺ Ways to Deliver a Prophecy

- 3 Sections to a Prophecy

- 5⁺ protocols to observe in prophesying

- 2 Characteristics of Personal Prophecy

- 2 Guide Posts for Sustained Growth In Prophesying

Servant Robin

You can Prophesy!

2021 EDITION

Published by SERVANT BOOKS www.servantministries.co.uk

Copyright © 2012 Robin Jegede-Brimson
No part of this book may be reproduced or transmitted in any form or by any means, electronic, mechanical, photocopying and recording or by any information storage and retrieval system without written permission from the author.

All scripture quotations, unless otherwise indicated, are taken from the Holy Bible, New International Version®, NIV®. Copyright ©1973, 1978, 1984, 2011 by Biblica, Inc.™ Used by permission of Zondervan. All rights reserved worldwide. www.zondervan.com. The "NIV" and "New International Version" are trademarks registered in the United States Patent and Trademark Office by Biblica, Inc.™

"Scripture quotations taken from the Amplified® Bible, Copyright © 1954, 1958, 1962, 1964, 1965, 1987 by The Lockman Foundation. Used by permission." (www.Lockman.org)

AFRICA
Henry Hamilton
Servant Ministries Nigeria
U.I.P.O. Box 22974, Ibadan, Nigeria.
Tel +234 080 3368 1552.
E–mail: hamiltonh78@hotmail.com

EUROPE
Robin Jegede-Brimson
Servant Ministries
7, Belton Close, Whitstable, Kent CT5 4LG, UK
Tel +44 0787 202 4364
E–mail: GodsOyster@aol.com

Cover design by
BARLT GRAPHICS PRINTS, NIG.
+234(0) 70 3822 8234
topekanbi@yahoo.com

To my friends –
Martin Bentley, Michael "Schambach" Oludipe,
Richard Mitchell, Lyndall Bywater and many
others who continue to provide a safe haven for
growth in pursuit of prophecy and the
prophetic ministry

ENDORSEMENTS

The prophet requires a baptised imagination seasoned with sanctified common sense. This booklet has plenty of both and comes out of Robin's deep desire to see the gift of prophecy released to do its distinctive work – building up God's people for the sake of God's world
Steve Coneys
Team Vicar, St Alphege, Seasalter
Team Rector, Whitstable Team Ministry

I love Robin's heart for Jesus. His unabashed passion for Jesus' mission undeniable and inspiring
Jim Denison
Team Leader, Canterbury Vineyard

A man's words hold no more value than his character. If his character is not good, I have a very difficult time hearing his words. Robin is a man of God that I have had the opportunity to spend considerable time with. Not only with him, but his family also - wife, children, and parents. He is a man of character in the home and away from the home; with his wife, with his children, and with his parents. He has a hunger for God, he is a man of prayer, and he has the fire of God within. He is one that I would not hesitate to read what he has to say. He listens for the voice of God and carefully speaks as not to say the wrong words. He is not a man of arrogance but one of humility and of a teachable spirit. I recommend his writings based on the strength of character that he possesses. I know they have come from a heart of hunger to edify the body of Christ.

John Bailey
Evangelist and Missionary USA / Senegal

Knowing your call and where you fit into the jigsaw of ministry is a depth many Christian believers never grasp. Having worked and walked with Robin over 20 odd years has convinced me, he has found his place in ministry. Robin is a voice to this generation and it is a clear tone with which he declares the prophetic call. Humbled to say I have learnt a lot from him.

Pastor Tunde Babalola
National Officer, Church Planting, Redeemed Christian Church of God (RCCG) Ireland

PREFACE

"You can all prophesy one after the other" was Paul's call to his spiritual children in the church at Corinth. He had begun this topic in the chapter we now know as 1 Corinthians 12, to address a question about spiritual gifts. He went on to list nine of these gifts, delving a little into how they were released into the body of believers. Pausing mid-way, he expounded the greatest of attributes – love in chapter 13 of the same book, entrenching this requirement as our supreme motivating factor. Paul then completed his 'a-b-c' of spiritual gifts with a list of do's and don'ts when it came to the exercising of those spiritual gifts.

Chapter 14 however only deals with tongues, interpretation of tongues and prophecy. Paul never did get back to explain what the other six gifts he mentioned earlier were exactly. Why we wonder? Perhaps one of the reasons was because if the church could get 'a handle' on these three elementary gifts the others would more easily fall into place.

This little booklet is to help us contend for one of the gifts which Paul regarded as the most basic – the gift of prophecy.

In 1 Corinthians 14 we are encouraged to: -

i. Desire it (verse 1) and be eager for it (verse 39)
ii. Understand its value as an essential complimentary gift to speaking in tongues (verse 5)
iii. Be able to communicate spiritual messages clearly and effectively (verses 8, 12 & 19)
iv. Grasp the effectiveness of prophecy as a tool to draw the unreached into the kingdom (verses 24 &25).

Building on these foundations, this booklet goes on to list 70+ facts (more can be found in our training manual) about prophecy including 30+ reasons why every believer should prophesy.

PREFACE

"You can all prophesy one after the other" was Paul's call to his spiritual children in the church at Corinth. He had begun this topic in the chapter we now know as 1 Corinthians 12, to address a question about spiritual gifts. He went on to list nine of these gifts, delving a little into how they were released into the body of believers. Pausing mid-way, he expounded the greatest of attributes – love in chapter 13 of the same book, entrenching this requirement as our supreme motivating factor. Paul then completed his 'a-b-c' of spiritual gifts with a list of do's and don'ts when it came to the exercising of those spiritual gifts.

Chapter 14 however only deals with tongues, interpretation of tongues and prophecy. Paul never did get back to explain what the other six gifts he mentioned earlier were exactly. Why we wonder? Perhaps one of the reasons was because if the church could get 'a handle' on these three elementary gifts the others would more easily fall into place.

This little booklet is to help us contend for one of the gifts which Paul regarded as the most basic – the gift of prophecy.

In 1 Corinthians 14 we are encouraged to: -

i. Desire it (verse 1) and be eager for it (verse 39)
ii. Understand its value as an essential complimentary gift to speaking in tongues (verse 5)
iii. Be able to communicate spiritual messages clearly and effectively (verses 8, 12 & 19)
iv. Grasp the effectiveness of prophecy as a tool to draw the unreached into the kingdom (verses 24 &25).

Building on these foundations, this booklet goes on to list 70+ facts (more can be found in our training manual) about prophecy including 30+ reasons why every believer should prophesy.

A whole generation of believers has grown up only being introduced to tongues; it's time to press on and add this amazing gift to our repertoire of spiritual graces. We do no one any good by not stepping forward to claim what has rightfully been made available to us from the day of Pentecost!

One last thing, the question of, 'Do all prophesy?' (In the vein of 1 Corinthians 12:29 & 30). The answer is simple, seen in another question, 'Do all get to be saved? Do all accept Jesus as LORD and Saviour?' No, being the right answer, even though it is GOD's desire for all to be saved, not all will.

Why? They either do not desire it, or are not willing to accept the terms for it, or are ignorant of its availability or misinformed as to its relevance and life application. The same is true for receiving the baptism of The HOLY SPIRIT, speaking in tongues as well as prophecy. This booklet[1] is to answer in part, The FATHER's heart cry for all His children,

---

[1] More can be found in the Training Manual

Now about spiritual gifts, brothers, I do not want you to be ignorant. (NIV UK) or *'misinformed' (1 Corinthians 12:1)*

If you have doubts about where you are right now spiritually, at the back of the book there is a prayer that may be used to bring you into salvation (peace with GOD, your maker). Once you have this gift of eternal life there is another prayer you can pray to bring you into the experience of receiving the gift of the HOLY SPIRIT and the manifestations of The SPIRIT. The prayers are to help provide expression for what you feel in your heart.

The '+' signs after the numbers are there to remind us that there's so much more for us to move into! Let's step right up!

Cheers,

Robin Jegede-Brimson
Canterbury
March 30th 2012

Contents

PREFACE vii
Understanding the terms 1
30+ Reasons to Prophesy...................................5
10+ WAYS TO PREPARE FOR PROPHETIC WORDS AND ENCOUNTERS 19
10+ WAYS TO ACTIVATE 23
PROPHETIC GRACE 23
10+ WAYS TO OBTAIN A PROPHECY 27
10+ WAYS TO DELIVER A PROPHECY 33
4 SECTIONS TO A PROPHECY 37
5+ PROTOCOLS TO OBSERVE IN PROPHESYING 39
2+ CHARACTERISTICS OF PERSONAL PROPHECY..41
2 GUIDE POSTS TO SUSTAINED GROWTH IN PROPHESYING..43
ABOUT THE AUTHOR 50

Understanding the terms . .

"My people are destroyed from lack of knowledge" (Hosea 4:6)

So, before we begin, let's ask ourselves, 'So what is prophecy?'

- A word or act originating from the HOLY SPIRIT that encourages, builds up and comforts.

- A word or act that reveals or releases the heart and mind of GOD into a particular context or situation.

We get this definition from 1 Corinthians 14:3 "The one who prophesies speaks to people for their strengthening, encouraging and comfort"

'Prophecy is supernatural utterance in a known tongue. The Hebrew meaning of the phrase, "to prophesy" is to flow forth. It also carries with it

the thought: to bubble forth like a fountain, to let drop, to lift up, to tumble forth, and to spring forth. The Greek word that is translated "prophesy" means to speak to one another. So "prophesy" can mean to speak for GOD or be his spokesperson'
'The HOLY SPIRIT and His Gifts' by Kenneth Hagin, (pg 139)

'Prophetic ministry is to draw out of people what the Lord has already put in their hearts, not necessarily to try and input something new and fresh'
'Developing your Prophetic Gift' by Graham Cooke

Just to note here that Old Testament prophecy was often 'future-telling' - predicting future events if you like. New Testament prophecy emphasises more however 'forth-telling' i.e. releasing what is on the heart of GOD for now.

When a fact or aspect of otherwise 'hidden knowledge' is revealed in prophecy it is another gift, that of 'Word of Knowledge' which is in operation[2]. This 'piece of knowledge' could be about something from the past, in the present or even in the future.

A "word of wisdom" is an instruction emanating from The SPIRIT of GOD which when followed and carried out in faith triggers and releases the supernatural power of GOD. This can result in a healing, a flow of resources or any other type of miracle. Examples are when Elijah said to cast a stick into the water, told Naaman to bathe in the River Jordan, or when JESUS told Peter to fish for a coin. It is the supernatural wisdom and direction of GOD to bring solutions in life.

This is different from walking in wisdom or acquiring general wisdom from the SPIRIT of GOD. Spiritual gifts by definition are by the prompting of The HOLY SPIRIT, we do not walk in them 24/7 but only as He wills.

These two revelatory gifts often use prophecy as a vehicle to release them.

It is GOD's will for every believer to prophesy.

___

This is in partial fulfilment of Joel's prophecy quoted by Peter –

"I will pour out my Spirit on all people. Your sons and daughters will prophesy, your old men will dream dreams, your young men will see visions. Even on my servants, both men and women, I will pour out my Spirit in those days. (Joel 2:28)

30⁺ Reasons to Prophesy

1. Comfort

Top of my list has to be we prophesy because when we do so we release comfort. The presence of The COMFORTER is made real and known and tangible as we release His word into people's lives. Prophesy to minister comfort! *"The LORD is with you, He has a plan for you, you are graven on the palm of His hand, He will never leave you nor forsake you etc."*

2. Eagerly desire

Paul very clearly tells us to desire basic spiritual gifts; to develop an appetite for them. It's not for us to say; 'Aw that's not really my thing' rather we are to pursue them in obedience to the dictates of scripture. (1 Corinthians 14:1).

Be eager to prophesy. This sounds like we are to jump at the opportunity to do so!
(1 Corinthians 14: 39).

Strong's Concordance defines 'zeloo' the Greek word translated 'eager' as *"to burn with zeal, to be heated or to boil with envy, hatred, anger, in a good sense, to be zealous in the pursuit of good"*!

3. A great compliment to speaking in tongues

Yea, tongues is a great means to edify and build ourselves up, get into spiritual warfare and so forth, yes; BUT . . . let's not forget about prophesying too! (1 Corinthians 14: 5).

4. Grace

You can do it Impartation of Grace

As we speak the word of the LORD to the saints we impart grace. Grace to do what they could not do before. Grace to prevail, grace to pursue. Grace to overcome.

5. Strength

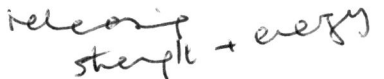

"Let the weakling say, 'I am strong'" (Joel 3:10) Ha Ha! Through the prophetic word strength comes to the weary soul. *"Now I commit you to God and to the word of his grace, which can build you up and give you an inheritance among all those who are sanctified"* (Acts 20:32) To strengthen and affirm.

6. Divine Recovery & Restoration

There was a time David was weary, he was at his wits end. (1 Samuel chapter 30) He sought for the word of the LORD, as it came it assured him that he should press on. All he lost was restored to him in the ensuing battle – because he received the prophetic word. The prophetic word released through you will empower generals and giants to rise up to reclaim lost ground! It will raise tired and weary souls back into their places!

7. Courage

"I give you this instruction in keeping with the prophecies once made about you, so that by

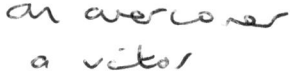

following them you may fight the good fight," (1 Timothy 1:18) Aha! As we remember the words spoken courage seeps into our hearts like waters into a dry well.

8. Life

It brings life. Prophecy brought life to the valley of dry bones (Ezekiel 37:1-4). Prophetic words are not ordinary 'psyching up' or 'pep talks'. No! They release the very life of GOD into dead situations! As the living 'rhema' of GOD's word is sent out!

9. Demonstrates love

The love chapter is right in the middle of the chat about spiritual gifts. Yes, so when we are full of love for people, how do we unbottle it? By prophesying over them!

10. Direction

"Let us go to the seer," said Saul's servant. He will tell us the way. Oh! How the church needs seers to point the way! Don't hold that unction back; don't shrink from declaring the word in

a word from the Lord.

You can Prophesy! 70 Truths about the Gift of Prophecy

your heart. As you release in humility all The SPIRIT has shown you, your faith will grow, your confidence will increase. Start today – promise yourself to speak and declare, your gift needs to be let out; it belongs to the church! *"Each one should use whatever gift he has received to serve others, faithfully administering God's grace in its various forms.* (1 Peter 4:10).

11. Conviction

As you speak conviction comes. (Acts 5:33, 7:54) your words carry the fire of GOD. *"Is not your word like fire in my bones"* said Jeremiah. Seek to release that which will bring others face to face with GOD Almighty here on earth before they get to heaven! "Sir, I perceive you are a prophet" she wriggled to get out of it, JESUS' words had hit their mark!

12. Reveals destiny

"Sovereign LORD, my eyes have seen your salvation . . .a light for revelation to the Gentiles" Luke 2:30-32. Simeon saw it and spoke it for the parents to hear. Prophetic

words are like bright shining torches that show the destiny of all, take time to hold meetings with your loved ones where you wait on The LORD to receive prophetic words and pictures for all your young ones. Give them something to hold onto, something that goes ahead of them like a light in a dark place, that lets them know that before they were born The FATHER knew them and had a plan for them. Speak into the lives of all your children! You can do this.

13. Releases from curses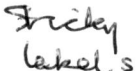

A curse can be a harsh or unkind word that has kept someone down for years. As you come alongside them YOUR WORD can set them free and release them to pursue GOD in their calling once again. Don't be afraid to release people, many are stooped down and bound waiting for that word to empower and release! Will you be used?

14. Gives vision

Prophecy gives spiritual vision. The Bible says, *"Where there is no vision, the people perish."* The Lord gives vision through the prophetic word (Proverbs 29:13,18). As you see for someone else you cause them to see for the first time in their lives. Be their eyes, their ears. Write what you hear from The LORD and show them.

15. Exercise spiritual senses

"What do you see?" Jeremiah was asked. Why? Because he needed to learn to see; *"You have seen well . . ."* If you don't try something you won't learn it, it's that simple! *"By reason of use"* (Hebrews 5:14) Exercise what you have.

16. Faith grows

The more you prophesy, confidence + faith

We prophesy according to our present level of faith[3] (Romans 12:6). Where does faith come into it? We all wonder at times, 'is that from my head or from The LORD? We learn to doubt what we perceive, but we also grow as we get it right! Trust more in GOD's ability to keep you than the devil's ability to deceive you! Exercise your faith! "My sheep hear my voice" assures

---

[3] Prophecy Manual (pg 15)

The MASTER, that includes you, yes you! (John 10:27).

17. Reveals GOD's mind

Heaven's perspective on a matter is made known as we tune into The HOLY SPIRIT. We have GOD's word, the Bible, to guide us on all the foundational principles but there will be those circumstances where we simply do not know what to do – to stay in the situation or to venture forward? The prophetic word releases the heart of GOD on a matter.

18. Reveals GOD's heart

How does FATHER feel about me? What about that sin from years back? Does He truly love me in spite of it all? Yes, PAPA's love comes through under prophetic unction. You can reveal the mind and tenderness of GOD through your hug. Through your 'weeping, with one who weeps', they can get to know GOD cares and they matter.

19. Releases Divine Strategy

"Shall we pursue?" In every major battle David would ask, "What shall we do?", "How do we go about this?" the answer would come, *"Make a compass around them".* The prophets would ask the same and receive the strategy, *"Dig ditches".* How could we be so presumptuous to battle without first hearing from The LORD?

20. Restores people's dignity and self respect

Have you ever felt nobody thinks you will amount to anything? Have you been trodden down, pushed about and beaten over? GOD sees the good in you, the lion in you, the one He made to show His Glory. As we receive prophecy and give prophecy light begins to shine and self worth is restored. You're great! You're tailor made for a purpose! You are called to shine! Stand up into the new you ☺

21. Releases the glory of GOD

Something happens to the atmosphere when a prophetic word is brought. Heaven reaches down and kisses the earth. It is as if The One who is speaking through vessels of clay despatches His angels to accompany the word.

22. Barren land is made fruitful

Where the prophetic word is made known a river flows, this river brings healing to the land. (Revelation 22:1-3) That which was once barren and cursed receives life. The creation is affected as we speak to it!

23. Moves the saints into position

"From him the whole body, joined and held together by every supporting ligament, grows and builds itself up in love, as each part does its work"(Ephesians 4:16)

Prophetic words move people into their callings and positions. As they ministered to The LORD, the word came, *"While they were worshipping the Lord and fasting, the Holy Spirit said, Set apart for me Barnabas and Saul for the work to which I have called them"* (Acts 13:2). What if they had no prophetic word? Would Paul have gone out? They needed the word to place them in their missionary role.

24. Makes spiritual messages clear and unambiguous.

". . . if the trumpet does not sound a clear call, who will get ready for battle?" (1 Corinthians 14:8) Often we may sense something deep down inside but not be able to articulate it. This is the function of prophesying, to make clear and intelligible, so that people may know what is being said and then work out what to do.

25. Releases a prayer agenda

We're not called to pray like a shot in the dark. Just like Elijah we are called to be like smart bombs that know exactly where the enemy is trying to launch an attack on the church.
(2 Kings 6:12) We are called to know where to pray strength into our lives. This comes from prophesying.

26. Stimulates growth

"So the elders of the Jews built, and they prospered through the prophesying of Haggai the prophet and Zechariah the son of Iddo. And they built and finished it, according to the commandment of the God of Israel, and according to the command of Cyrus, Darius, and Artaxerxes king of Persia" (Ezra 6:14) (KJV) They needed the words of the prophets to complete what they had once laid aside.

27. To press into the higher revelatory gifts.

Our eyes become more open to the realm of the unseen. As we step out in faith and release that first bit of prophecy more opens up before us! We can then press into words of knowledge, words of wisdom and the discerning of spirits.

28. Reveals the bigger picture!

That bit of the picture, which was previously hidden, now also becomes known. We are all given to see a bit of the larger cause and will and strategy of heaven. Don't ever despise your little bit!

29. Reaches the unreached!

We need to further grasp its effectiveness as a tool to draw the unreached into the kingdom. If they come in and we are prophesying someone will have a word for them! A word that will let them know GOD loves them and knows them individually! Wow! (1 Corinthians 14: 24, 25).

30. Releases a 'spirit of prophesy'

atmosphere changes

The more people prophesy and yield themselves to The SPIRIT of GOD, the more likelihood a 'spirit of prophecy', a tangible prophetic atmosphere, can fall on a place. When this happens it is very exciting – anyone who steps into that region becomes affected. I have seen this a few times, once while ministering with others at London's Trafalgar Square! This is what was going on when Saul sent men to try to arrest David. They were simply inundated with the spirit of prophecy. (1 Samuel 19: 18-24)

NOTES

10+ WAYS TO PREPARE FOR PROPHETIC WORDS AND ENCOUNTERS

1. By responding to His calling in our hearts and drawing away from our normal routine for the day. Hear His whispers – take time off.

2. By responding to something we have seen that has attracted our attention. Ask yourself, 'Was that meant to happen?' 'Could that have been avoided?' 'Why did they get that

blessing and not me?' (Exodus 3, Moses and the burning bush)

3. Have you had a repeated dream? Or a distinct impression about something when you woke up? Most often GOD waits for us to respond first before more is released.

4. Worship. Entering the Presence of GOD in new depths of intimacy. Love your GOD with all your heart, soul and mind! Love Him. Choose to honour the worship and praise time in your church meetings. Don't ever be an average worshipper. In your heart go to the limit.

5. Soaking. Cultivating and abiding in an atmosphere of worship. Stay there. Wait until you begin to see. This could be in times of soaking prayer as well as soaking worship, quiet or mellow.

6. Speaking in tongues. This prepares your heart to hear. Learn to keep speaking

until you hear. Press in, press on, remove the limits.

7. Reading the Bible for energy. Speed reading 10 – 15 chapters can strengthen your inner man help to prepare you for prophetic experiences.

8. By dwelling (meditating) on passages containing prophetic encounters. For example Revelation 1:10, Zechariah 1 and Ezekiel 1 – these are all in-roads and pathways to enter into those same realms of heavenly visitation.

9. By removing fear of what if? Trust His power to keep you abundantly more than the enemy's power to deceive you.

10. By renewing your mind in the word of GOD. GOD wants to use your imagination in incredible ways to help you see! This is 'the eyes of your heart' (Ephesians 1:18). So, don't allow your mind to dwell on anything you know GOD would not have you dwell on –

steer it away into things pleasant, pure, praiseworthy (Philippians 4:8)

11. By not walking alone. Find your prophetic teammates and players. Share experiences, swop notes, encourage one another. Find those not jealous or intimidated by your gifts and revelations. Don't walk alone, find who you need to walk with.

12. Read the manuals and biographies of those who GOD has used in prophetic ministry. Learn from them. A whole lot better than letting experience be your only teacher, odds are – you'll run out of time!

NOTES

10+ WAYS TO ACTIVATE PROPHETIC GRACE

1. By putting on a cloak of humility. A mindset that says, 'LORD if I get it right it is for Your glory, if I get it wrong it is for my learning'.

2. By activating faith by breathing in a fresh breath of The HOLY SPIRIT. An act that says, 'Here goes LORD! ' (Reminds me of when I used to psyche myself up before plunging from a 10 meter diving board).

3. By opening our eyes to observe what the HOLY SPIRIT is highlighting. "What

or who is 'standing out' to me?' It is much the same as the way we read the scriptures and a particular passage stands out. We can grow 'on purpose' in our sensitivity to The HOLY SPIRIT and his promptings. This often is what someone is wearing, clothing, jewellery.

4. By focusing on, or being drawn to what someone is wearing. Often as a particular tunic or colour someone is wearing is highlighted leading us to a connection in our knowledge of what that colour means. For example, Purple is royalty, Plum is new wine, Blue is the river of GOD and revelation, Light blue is heavens or The HOLY SPIRIT and Red is the fire of GOD, healing and anointing.

5. By recalling a memory. This often means that what we saw can be repeated. This is the hidden power of a testimony. The HOLY SPIRIT works along with our minds.

6. From a picture that flashes across our minds. It is seen in our imagination, which is GOD's primary means of speaking with us. As we hone in on it, it develops and its meaning becomes clearer.

7. By being made aware of a Bible character that can then link into the person you are to prophesy to.

8. By the knowledge of a Bible phrase being recalled. My most used and personal favourite is Jeremiah 29:11-13 *"I know the plans . . ."*

9. By the knowledge of a Bible character being recalled. Commonly used are David, (after GOD's heart) .."

10. By singing in the sprit or singing a new song to The LORD. This stimulates prophetic flow.

NOTES

10+ WAYS TO OBTAIN A PROPHECY

1. **By seeing in the spirit**. This is a very common way of receiving messages from The SPIRIT. This could be a word, a picture, a drawing, a colour, a shape. It is from The LORD, grow in your confidence.

2. **By hearing in the spirit**. We have inner spiritual ears as well as physical ears. Our spirit is capable of all the five senses our physical body has. We learn to discern the voice of The HOLY SPIRIT as well as our own spirit. Sometimes we will not hear The HOLY SPIRIT but The LORD's audible voice.

3. **By having a flow of thoughts**. Not all people see pictures or hear voices as

often as others do. For some the major channel through which prophetic words come is by having strong thoughts. Your mind and imagination are not your enemy! The term 'eyes of your heart' referred to in the prayer from Ephesians 1:17-21 comes from a Greek word, *deanoyah* meaning mind, way of thinking. GOD speaks to you mostly in your mind; your imagination. So keep your mind pure or you will always wonder, was that me (i.e. your sinful nature) or my mind? All your thoughts must be what GOD is comfortable with. This explains Isaiah 55:10 – my thoughts higher than yours – He wants us to have and share His thoughts.

4. **By having a strong perception in your heart**. Paul would use the phrase, *"I perceive in my heart . . ."* Not all prophetic words have to begin with, *"Thus says The LORD . . ."* the more relaxed we are when giving a prophetic word the better. We should avoid things like clichés, trying to sound spiritual airs etc. It is much safer when a

word comes as an inner feeling to say, *"I perceive . . ."*

5. **By receiving a smell**. I have smelt both good smells associated with The Presence of GOD and also bad smells associated with either a lingering presence of evil or sin. I remember once my wife and I were visiting a church and she began to feel very uncomfortable. I asked what was wrong and she asked if there was a toilet door left open near by. Her spirit was picking up an offensive smell of a toilet yet there was none around. The LORD was letting us know that something was wrong with this otherwise healthy looking church.

6. **By what your body senses**. This is how a word of knowledge for healing often flows, it is you being aware of something GOD wants to do.

7. **From an awareness of GOD's creation**. His creation speaks and declares (Psalm 19) Listen.

8. **By declaring a 'NOW' word**. As you team up with The HOLY SPIRIT a word drops in your heart, which you then release. Example is Elijah's word when the king was about to cut off his head. (2 Kings 7:1). So we speak forth a faith-filled and SPIRIT-led declaration.

9. **By operating in discerning of spirits**. How this works is your eyes are opened to see something that is present in the spiritual realm. This could be healing hovering over a person, or an angel that has suddenly appeared on the scene. When these things happen it is because The HOLY SPIRIT wants you to work with what you have been shown to bring about a miracle.

10. **By receiving a burden**. Allow your heart to be moved by The HOLY SPIRIT, carry GOD The FATHER's burden for a situation. As this comes on you it is an indication that GOD wants to use you in this situation.

NOTES

10+ WAYS TO DELIVER A PROPHECY

" . . . .be eager to prophesy . . . But everything should be done in a fitting and orderly way"
1 Corinthians 14:39-40

We are told to be *"effective stewards of the manifold grace of GOD"* (1 Peter 4:10). So find your prophetic niche. How you best hear GOD. How you flow best in the prophetic. Learn it, study it, and increase in grace in it by being sensitive and diligent.

1. **By speaking**. *"Speak as the oracles of GOD"* (1 Peter 4:11) (KJV). Some people have great voices when it comes to releasing a word from The FATHER. It is important that we catch and reflect the emotion of GOD as we do this not our emotions.

2. **In a song**. Sometimes a tune will come with the prophetic word. It is as if the tune 'carries' in a lifting sort of way, the word to be released.

3. **By playing a musical instrument**. The heart of GOD can be felt as certain people play. They release the atmosphere and presence of GOD into a place. The sounds they play release a spirit of prophesy. As people come under that they being to prophesy. Sometimes it is as if The HOLY SPIRIT is trying to say something to us through the musical instruments!

4. **As a drawing, sketch or painting**. We speak by faith, we can also begin to draw by faith, we receive the first line of inspiration and gather what The HOLY SPIRIT desires to release as we gently go along. At the end the picture speaks – and it is there for the recipient to take home.

5. **In a drama sketch**. The heart and mind of GOD can be powerfully portrayed in drama. Directed by HOLY SPIRIT.

6. **By writing it down**. Sometimes there is no occasion to deliver a word by word of mouth. It can be just as powerful, more so even, in written form. Learn to carry a notebook with you wherever you go. Treasure prophetic words.

7. **As a recording**. Most mobile phones today have a recording setting – get to know it. The advantage of a recording is that it carries the emotion and sense of what was said. It captures what would otherwise have been lost or distorted by our poor memory banks.

8. **In prayer**. All prayer ought to be prophetic, by this I mean, originating from the heart of God as revealed by The HOLY SPIRIT. *"Who has known the mind of GOD?"* (1Corinthians 2:10 –16) Our prayers should carry this sense of discovery about the plan of GOD; they should unveil mystery.

9. **In dance and waving of banners and flags**. As HOLY SPIRIT anoints you, flow with Him, allow expression to come in a naturally supernatural way.

10. **With your emotions**. By laughing, by crying. GOD laughs! Sometimes that settles a matter. By weeping. This can be a release into a new birthing of something new.

11. **In a prophetic action** – by doing something as you are prompted to by HOLY SPIRIT. Examples of this could be washing the feet of GOD's saints, feeding the poor, buying a new pair of shoes for someone, showing unusual levels of kindness etc.

NOTES

4 SECTIONS TO A PROPHECY

The revelation – what precisely has come to you? What have you seen or heard? What has The HOLY SPIRIT shown you? Define it; encapsulate it using your own natural thought processes. Grasp the start of the flow and its ending.

The interpretation – so, what precisely does this mean? Sometimes a 'Word of Wisdom' will accompany the revelation in which case the interpretation and application will come with it. At other times we need to tread gently and ask questions – 'Are there references to what I saw in the Bible?' 'Does someone else understand the meaning of what I saw?' 'Do I need to take time off to seek for the meaning?' Etc

The application – OK, I have the first two, now what is the best way forward? Again it is great when a word of wisdom comes it solves these questions for us. Otherwise we need to take time to ask for wisdom – how to correctly apply knowledge.

The delivery – with the appropriate sensitivity and emotion; with humility and an accurate reflection of your perceptions.

NOTES

5+ PROTOCOLS TO OBSERVE IN PROPHESYING

1. Don't presume that the person is happy to receive your prophetic word. Be gracious in seeking permission.

2. Wherever possible let a third person be around when delivering a word. If a lady, ask if her husband is around and vice-versa

3. Where you can, ask for your word to be validated. 'Did that fit somewhere?'

4. Never use it to get a private or personal point across!

5. Do ask for permission before you follow through with prayer

6. When a prophecy is given in a group setting, the leader of the group ought always to respond appropriately in prayer; it is rude to ignore it.

2+ CHARACTERISTICS OF PERSONAL PROPHECY

1. It is incomplete. We all see in part, never everything.

2. It is conditional[4]. Always determinant on your appropriate response to GOD.

NOTES

2 GUIDE POSTS TO SUSTAINED GROWTH IN PROPHESYING

LOVE

1. Let your motive be love and service. It is never about you, it is about serving humanity in the cause of Christ. The gifts are given "for the common good" (1Corithians 12:7). Keep your eyes on 1Corthians 13. The greatest is love.

HUMILITY

2. Stay humble and simple. Those with marked prophetic grace are called to use it to equip the saints (Ephesians 4:11-13) not to draw attention to themselves. Never presume to reach a place of infallibility in your privileged flow in the prophetic. Humility is a garment we are called to put on daily by choice. Don't leave home without it.

NOTES

PRAYERS

A prayer to receive JESUS as your LORD, and SAVIOUR from sin and its consequences – separation from GOD and judgement

Dear LORD JESUS,

I believe that you died on the cross for me. I believe that you died in my place for all my sins, all that I have done wrong. I thank You that You loved me enough to give Your life as a sacrifice for mine. I receive your love for me right now; I ask that you take away my sins and all that has been wrong in my life. Please wash me clean and come to live in my heart. I accept you as my LORD and Saviour. Thank you for saving me, for coming into my heart and life. I love you and receive the eternal life that You give right now. Thank You LORD JESUS! Amen.

A prayer to receive the baptism of The HOLY SPIRIT and His gifts

Dear FATHER-GOD,

I thank you for sending JESUS; I have received as my LORD and Saviour. Thank You that I now qualify for Your promise to me to also be filled with the power of The HOLY SPIRIT. I come to You on the basis of Your Word, the Bible, and right now ask You to fill me, drench me and flood me to overflowing with Your precious gift of the HOLY SPIRIT.

HOLY SPIRIT I receive You into my life now in a unique, personal, powerful and special way. Thank You, as You fill me, for the gifts You also have for me especially the divine ability to speak in other tongues and prophesy. I ask for, and believe You for these gifts to show up in my life right away! Thank You my FATHER! Thank You LORD JESUS! Thank You precious and dear HOLY SPIRIT! Amen.

Other books by the same author

1. **LEST WE FORGET** – The life and times of the pioneer missionaries to Ibadan, Nigeria (1851 – 1868) As a young girl Anna's dream was to one day be a martyr for JESUS. This is the powerful story of her life along with her husband David, who were the first Christian missionaries to Ibadan in South West Nigeria from 1851 to 1868. As you read it you will be impacted by a life on fire for GOD!

2. **THE WELLS OF OUR FATHERS -** A history of revival in southwest Nigeria from 1830 to 1959. But this is far more than a history lesson, this is about honouring the lives of all who have gone before us and laid foundations. It is on these foundations that we stand and ascend to the next levels of faith and reformation that The HOLY SPIRIT has in store for us. Life and grace are released as we honour these generals, prophets and apostles who have preceded us. We owe them.

3. **TRANSITION** – Something new is on the horizon! Highlighting areas that The HOLY SPIRIT is revealing to His saints where emphasis

and change are needed to break old moulds and be supple to be able to contain the new wine falling on the church. This book starts off with a list of 25 such areas then hones in on six of them including restoration of the prophetic and apostolic offices.

4. **CROSSOVER!** – A manual for transcending societal & cultural obstacles for maximum impact. This book is a reminder of the love The FATHER has for the cultures and nations of the world. Featuring practical ways for social contextulisation including how to conduct socially open church services and contemporary evangelistic paradigms. The FATHER's love is portrayed for us as individuals freeing us to our unique and precious identities.

5. **YOU CAN PROPHESY! 70 truths about the gift of prophecy -** A handy and concise resource covering 22 Reasons to Prophesy, 7 Ways to Prepare for Prophetic Words and Encounters, 7 Ways to Activate Prophetic Grace and loads more. This book presents prophesy as a gift available to every believer, it is not a mark of some great level or height of spirituality.

6. **TRAINING & ACTIVATION MANUALS** – *Equipping the saints (Ephesians 4:11)* - Three resources for training in all righteousness that the man of GOD may be fully equipped in primary areas of the faith. – *Equipping the saints (Ephesians 4:11)*

   a. **25 types of Prayer, Tongues and Interpretation** – all in one manual. LORD teach us to pray was the cry of the disciples, 'LORD make it ours too!'

   b. **Prophecy and Prophetic Ministry** – this gift belongs to us! It is not just for the super saint! Covering all the basics you need to walk in prophecy as your spiritual inheritance.

   c. **Faith, Working Of Miracles & Gifts Of Healings – 21 ways GOD heals today!**

ABOUT THE AUTHOR

Robin, a Nigerian Englishman, runs *Servant Ministries*, an equipping ministry that operates through teaching, preaching, book writing and conferences. He is the convener of the *Inter Prophetic Apostolic Alliance* (IPAA), a coalition of apostolic and prophetic ministers running with a vision to be a voice to the nations and the re-establishment of apostolic structure. He also leads the *Nigeria Academy of Prophetic & Apostolic Reform* (NAPAR).

Robin is passionate to see the church transition to the 'new' that GOD desires to accomplish around the world. In July 1996 Robin received a vision for mission's fires in Nigeria, Africa &

Europe. Since then he has been in active pursuit of GOD for a move of the HOLY SPIRIT that will trigger this and other events. In December 1999 in obedience to a divine call he immigrated to the UK as a 'return missionary'.

Robin is the author of "THE BLAZE OF TRANSITION" as well as several manuals on prophetic ministry and books on revival (see amazon.co.uk). His ministry (S.M) is part of "Churches in Communities" led by Dr Hugh Osgood; he is commissioned as a prophet under IPAA as well as "Christian International Europe" (CIE) led by Dr Sharon Stone. He is a spiritual son of Apostle Mosy Madugba (MPN).

Robin releases a monthly "Word for the month" on YouTube ("Robin Jegede-Brimson"). He worships and serves at various churches that he is relationally connected with across London & Kent.

He is an avid squash player and loves spending time in his garden. He is married to Nyema, a worshipper and prophetic intercessor passionate about the ministry of healing. They are blessed with four grown up children and enjoy the grace of GOD living in the seaside town of Whitstable, Kent.